# WHEN

# Did dinosaurs rule the earth?

Om KIDZ
An imprint of Om Books International

# Contents

## When did dinosaurs rule the Earth?

About 200 million years ago! Dinosaurs were a group of reptiles that lived during the Mesozoic Era, which began 245 million years ago. They were the dominant life-forms on Earth for nearly 180 million years. But they faced a sudden extinction at the end of the Cretaceous period, about 65 million years ago.

**Pocket fact**

A large number!
Around 1,543-2,468 dinosaur species existed on Earth during the Mesozoic Era.

**Find out**

What was the Earth like when dinosaurs lived on it?

## When was the first dinosaur fossil found?

Way back in 1676! Robert Plot the curator of an English museum found a thigh bone that he thought belonged to a giant. But that fossil disappeared without a trace. Later on, in 1822, Mary Ann Mantell and her husband Gideon discovered the large teeth of the herbivorous reptile Iguanodon, in England.

## When was the name 'dinosaur' coined?

In 1841! Richard Owen, an English biologist, anatomist and palaeontologist is remembered for coining the word *Dinosauria*, meaning "Terrible Reptile" or "Fearfully Great Reptile". He published an important general account of the land reptiles of the Mesozoic Era and stated that dinosaur fossils were distinct from the teeth or bones of any living creature; and hence he named the group Dinosauria. He divided them into three categories—the carnivorous Megalosaurus, the herbivorous Iguanodon and the armoured Hylaeosaurus.

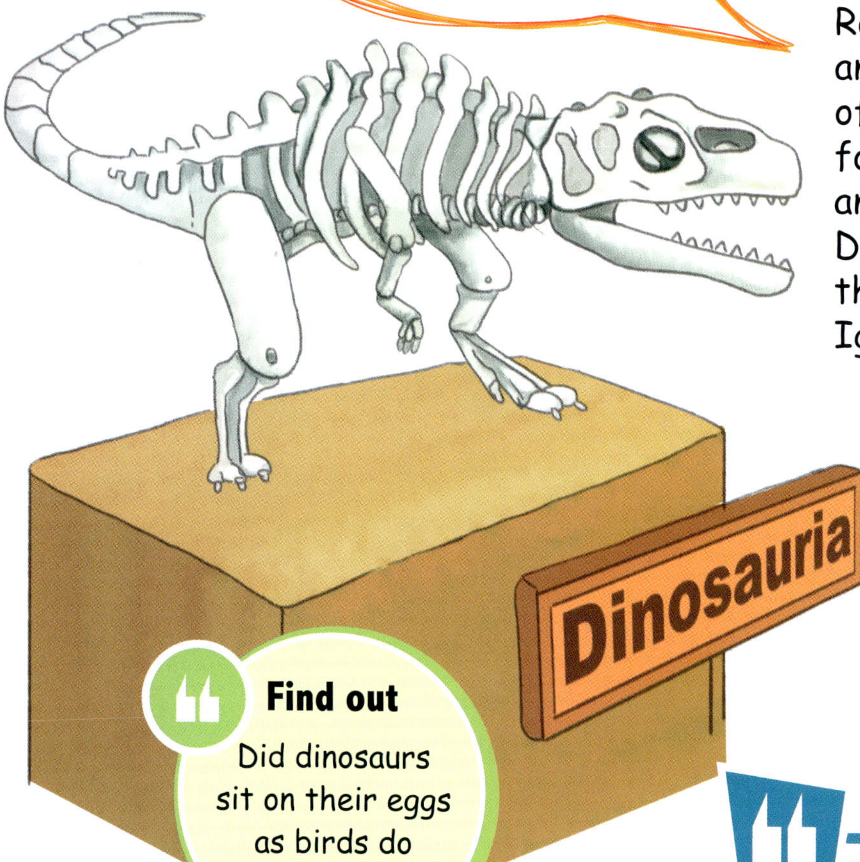

**Find out**

Did dinosaurs sit on their eggs as birds do today?

**Pocket fact**

**Dawn Stealer!**

The earliest named dinosaur was the meat-eating Eoraptor and its name means "dawn stealer". It was named so because it lived at the dawn of the Dinosaur Age.

## When were the massive eggs of Therizinosaurus found?

In 2011! A nursery of Therizinosaurus was found in the Gobi Desert in Mongolia by the palaeontologist Yoshitsugu Kobayashi and his colleagues. The nesting colony had 17 clutches of eggs. The eggs were round and 5-inches in diameter with rough outer shells. The eggs did not harbour dinosaur embryos but many of them had holes with eggshells inside. It seemed as if a baby dinosaur had poked a hole in the egg and the broken shells had fallen back inside.

## When was the nearly-complete skeleton of a dinosaur found?

In 1988! The fossil of a nearly-complete skeleton of a bipedal dinosaur named Herrerasaurus was found in north-western Argentina in the foothills of the Andes. Herrerasaurus was one of the earliest dinosaurs that lived 231 million years ago. The fragments of this fossil were discovered by Victorino Herrera, an Andean goatherd, in 1959. However, it was in 1988 that Alfredo Monetta discovered the rest of the bones of the Herrerasaurus, and this gave the researchers a complete picture of the dinosaur.

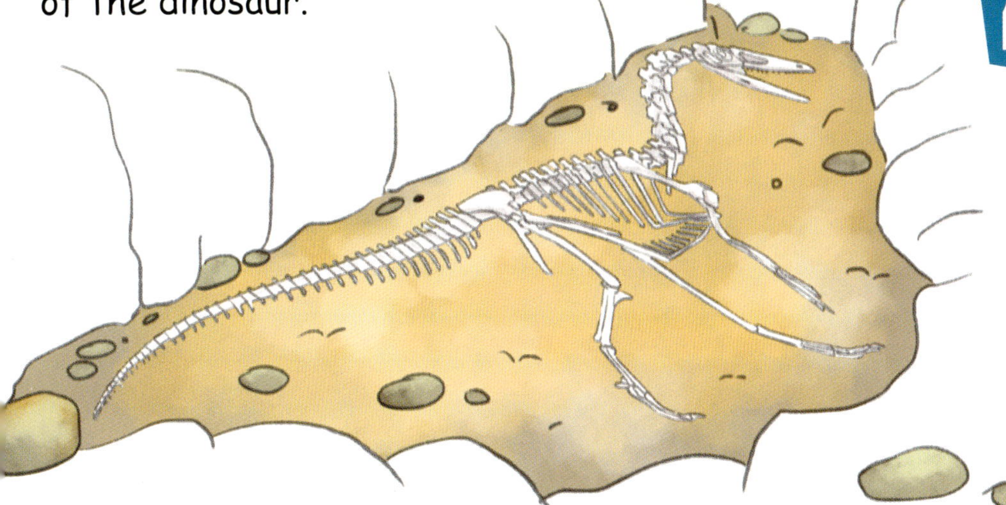

### Pocket fact

**Double hinged!**
The Herrerasaurus had a long pointed head with sharp teeth enclosed in a double-hinged jaw. The joints in the jaw allowed the Herrerasaurus to grip its prey.

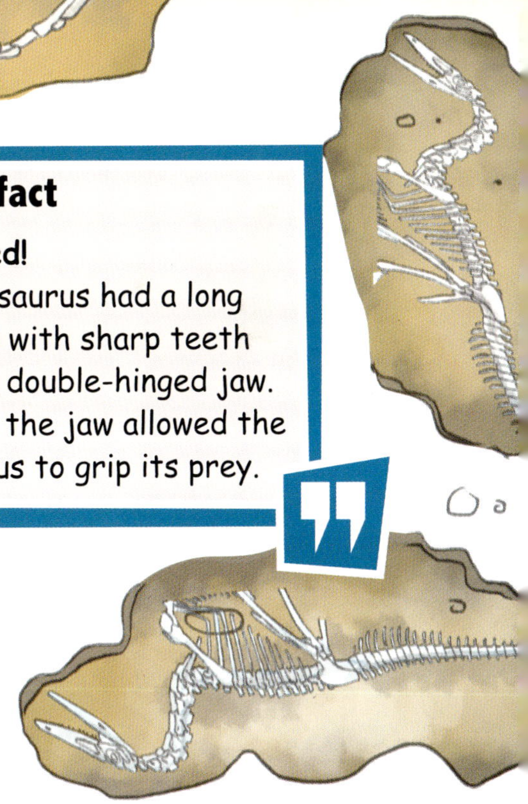

### Find out

Was Coelophysis a herbivore or a carnivore?

## When were hundreds of Coelophysis skeletons discovered?

In 1947! Edwin H. Colbert, curator of fossil reptiles at the American Museum of Natural History, was on an expedition to the Baldwin's Coelophysis site with his team. It was on this expedition that fossil preparatory George Whitaker found a bone-bed of hundreds of Coelophysis skeletons in the red Triassic rocks at Ghost Ranch near Abiquiu, New Mexico. This discovery made Coelophysis a popular dinosaur.

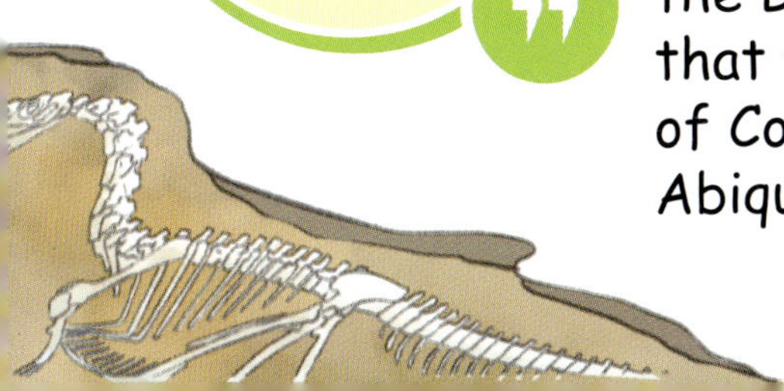

## When did the first giant dinosaur appear on Earth?

215-222 million years ago! Dinosaurs were not the first living things that roamed the Earth. Reptiles like Archosaurus, Pterosaurus and Desmatosuchus lived on Earth before dinosaurs came into existence. The appearance of dinosaurs dates back to the late Triassic period. Chindesaurus and Coelophysis were one of the earliest-known dinosaurs and they were around 6-8 feet in length. However, the first giant dinosaurs, the Plateosauruses, were around 26-feet long and 3-4 metres high.

**Find out**

Which was the largest known Sauropod?

**Pocket fact**

**Before the dinosaurs!**
Plateosaurus fossils were first discovered in France in 1837. It was actually named before dinosaurs were recognized as a group.

### When did Sauropods appear on Earth?

In the Late Triassic Era! Sauropods were lizard-hipped dinosaurs with very long necks, long tails, small heads (as compared to their body) and four thick, pillar-like legs. They were known for the huge sizes attained by some species. They were diversely and abundantly found 150-120 million years ago, during the Late Jurassic and Early Cretaceous periods.

## When did Theropods live on Earth?

From the Late Triassic Era through the latest Cretaceous Era! Theropods were ancestrally carnivores but later they evolved to become herbivores, omnivores, piscivores and insectivores. They first appeared approximately 231.4 million years ago. Theropods included a wide range of dinosaurs—from the smallest-known adult Mesozoic non-avian dinosaur to the great Tyrannosaurus and Giganotosaurus.

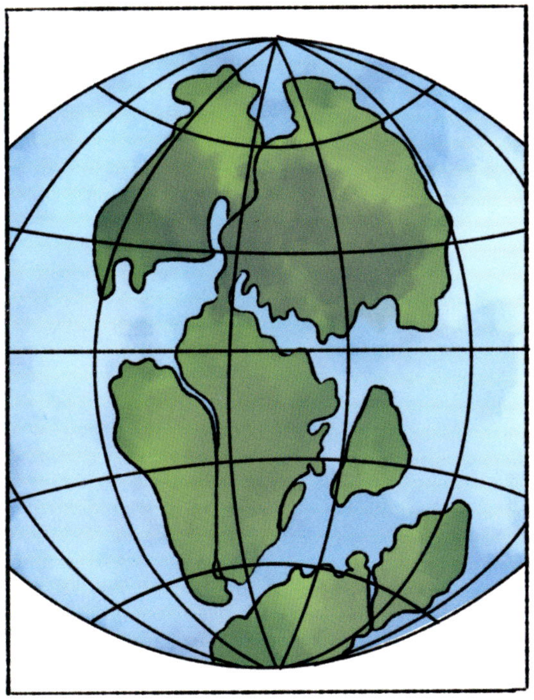

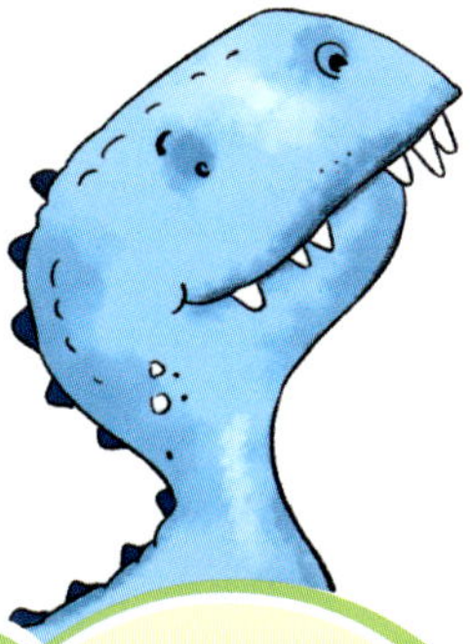

**Find out**

What was the size of a T. Rex's skull?

**Pocket fact**

**I am the smallest!**
Hesperonychus was the smallest-known North American carnivorous dinosaur. It was about 1-metre long. It ate insects, baby dinosaurs and small Cretaceous animals.

### When did the 'King of Dinosaurs' evolve?

In the late Jurassic period! The Jurassic period extended from 145 million to 201 million years ago. T. Rex, the king of dinosaurs appeared on Earth about 150 million years ago. It was a large meat-eating dinosaur, with very large, high skulls that were over 3 feet long. It weighed around 4000-7000 kg and was approximately 14-metres long.

## When did dinosaurs gather together in groups?

While hunting and also when they wanted to stay safe! Palaeontologists have found many dinosaur fossils which show social groups. It is assumed that plant-eaters (like Hypsilophodons) might have gathered in groups to protect themselves from their predators. On the other hand, carnivorous dinosaurs (like the Velociraptors) may have formed groups while hunting for food.

### Pocket fact

**Human-like fingers!**

The Iguanodon was not only known for its size and ungainly posture but also for its fingers. The most notable features of the Iguanodon were its hind limbs that were equipped with five fingers. Three of its middle fingers were bound together with flesh whereas the fourth finger and thumb were able to move freely.

### Try it!

What name would you like to use for a group of Diplodocuses?

## When was the first big hoard of dinosaur skeletons found?

In 1878! The first big hoard of skeletons was found 322 metres underground in a coal mine in Bernissart, Belgium. Miners were digging at 322 metres when they came across, relatively complete, 30 dinosaur skeletons, encrusted with pyrite. The discovery was reported to the Belgian Royal Museum of Natural History (as it was then known) on 12 April 1878.

## When was the smallest fossilized dinosaur skeleton found?

In the 1970s! The smallest fossilized dinosaur skeleton ever found was that of a baby Mussaurus's skull. Mussaurus was a small, plant-eating dinosaur. Palaeontologists have not found any adult Mussaurus fossils yet. During the 1970s, Jose Bonaparte, who was leading an expedition to the El Tranquilo Formation, discovered fragmented juvenile fossils, skulls and dinosaur eggs. The skulls of the baby dinosaurs were so small that they could fit on a fingertip!

**Find out**

How many dinosaur fossils are there in the Dinosaur National Park?

**Pocket fact**

**Thin egg shells!**
Mussaurus' eggs are known for having unusually thin shells as compared to most long-necked dinosaurs whose eggs had much thicker shells.

## When were 300 tons of dinosaur bones found?

In 1909! A palaeontologist, Earl Douglass was hunting for dinosaur fossils in Utah, USA, when he found eight tailbones of an Apatosaurus protruding from a sandstone hill in the Utah desert. This eventually led him to the discovery of a dinosaur quarry where approximately 300 tons of dinosaur bones were found. In 1915, the Dinosaur National Monument was established in Utah to protect and conserve this dinosaur quarry.

## When did the Ankylosaurus swing its club?

When it sensed danger! Ankylosaurus was a heavily armoured dinosaur that lived during the late Cretaceous period, about 65.5 million to 66.8 million years ago. It had a large club-like protrusion at the end of its tail. Ankylosaurus swung its club to hit its attackers. Alternatively, it may have been used for display purposes, such as for attracting mates.

**Find out**

When and by whom was Troodon first discovered?

**Pocket fact**

**Fused lizard!**

The name Ankylosaurus means "fused lizard". The dinosaur was named so because it had fused bones in its skull and other parts of its body. These bones gave the Ankylosaurus a rugged appearance, similar to a crocodile.

## When did a Troodon usually hunt for its prey?

At night! Troodon was a small, bird-like, meat-eating dinosaur that lived 76 million years ago, during the Campanian age of the Cretaceous period. It was considered to be one of the most intelligent dinosaurs, given the size of its brain. Palaeontologists believe that Troodon had large, forward-facing eyes and vertical pupils that granted it keen vision for hunting, even at night.

## When did a dinosaur fossil irritate its finders?

When they were unable to reconstruct its original features! Irritator was a dinosaur that lived around 105–110 million years ago, during the early Cretaceous period. Its only known fossil, an 80-cm skull was discovered in 1996 by palaeontologists Martill, Cruikshank, Frey, Small and Clarke. The fossil was badly masked by plaster, by illegal fossil hunters, making the snout appear longer. This made it difficult for the palaeontologists to reconstruct its original features and thus it was named Irritator—a name which comes from the word irritated.

### Pocket fact

**Not always static!**

Dinosaur names are not always static. The giant Apatosaurus was initially named so by palaeontologist Othniel C. Marsh. Later on, similar but larger bones of the Apatosaurus were found and so the dinosaur's name was changed to Brontosaurus. However, eventually, it was decided that the first-decided name "Apatosaurus" should be retained.

### Find out

How do palaeontologists preserve fossils?

## When was the first dinosaur brain discovered?

In 2004! The first fossilized dinosaur brain was discovered by amateur fossil hunter Jamie Hiscocks in Surrey, England. The brain belonged to the plant-eating dinosaur, Bexhill iguanodontian, that roamed in Sussex, England, a little over 130 million years ago. This is one of the most amazing dinosaur discoveries because of the rarity of the preservation of the soft-tissue of the dinosaur brain.

## When did the "Bone Wars" begin?

In 1870! The "Bone Wars" also known as the "Great Dinosaur Rush" refers to a period of intense fossil discovery by two palaeontologists. Edward Drinker Cope of the Academy of Natural Sciences, Philadelphia and Othniel Charles Marsh of Peabody Museum of Natural History, faced off in a very peculiar struggle. They competed to determine who could find more dinosaur bones and species. During this period, around 130 species were identified between the two rivals. The "Bone Wars" ended in 1897 with the death of Edward Drinker Cope.

**Find out**

Who won the "Bone Wars" and why?

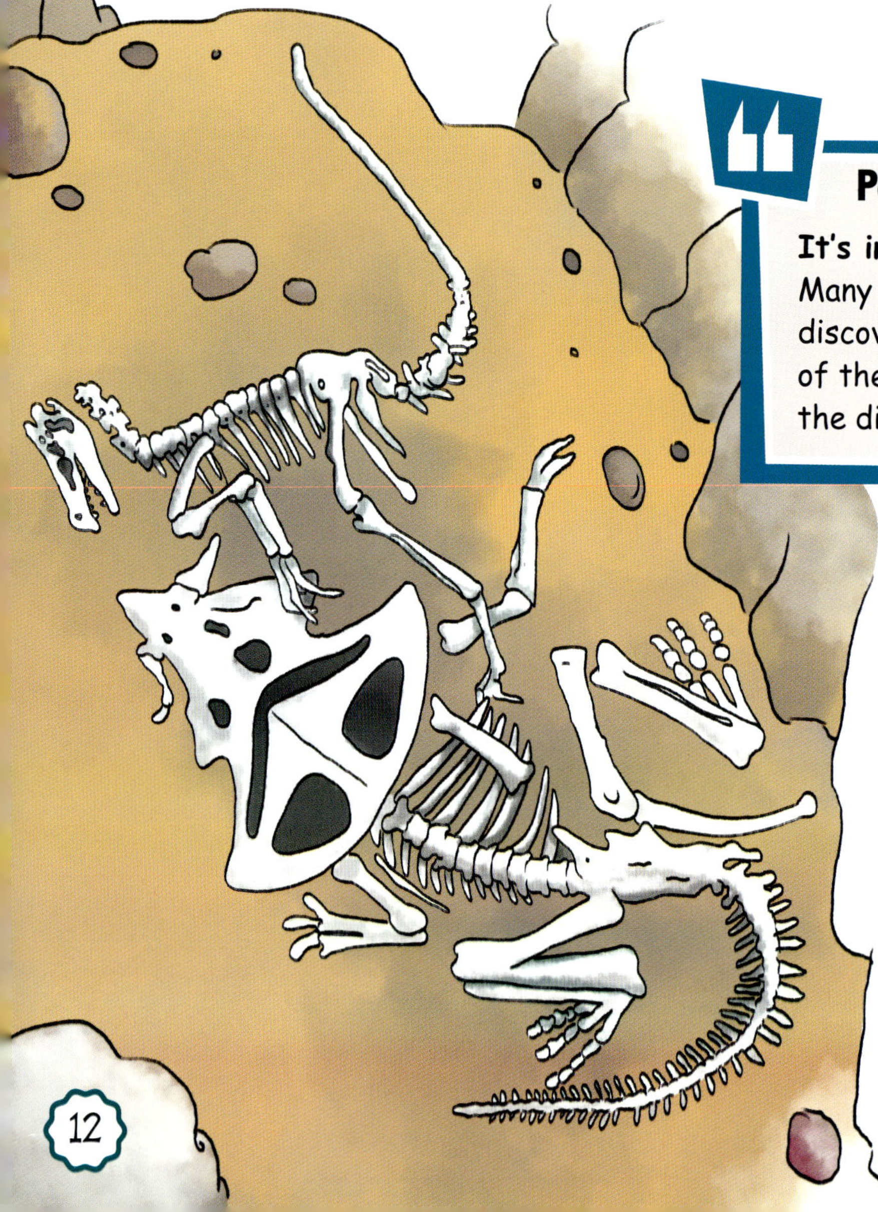

**Pocket fact**

**It's interesting!**

Many interesting dinosaur fossils have been discovered by palaeontologists till date. One of the most interesting fossils was that of the dinosaur Citipati shielding her eggs!

## When was the "Fighting Dinosaurs" fossil found?

In 1971! A Polish-Mongolian team discovered the fossils of a Velociraptor and a Protoceratops locked in combat, with both dinosaurs having died at the same time. The fossil shows one of the Velociraptor's foot claws lodged into the Protoceratops' neck, and the Protoceratops seems to have bit down and broken one of the Velociraptor's arms. This discovery showed that predatory dinosaurs hunted and scavenged the plant-eating dinosaurs.

## When was the first Velociraptor fossil discovered?

In 1923! Velociraptor was a theropod dinosaur that lived approximately 71-75 million years ago, during the later part of the Cretaceous period. Palaeontologist Peter Kaisen discovered the Velociraptor fossil on the first American Museum of Natural History expedition to the Outer Mongolian Gobi Desert. The fossil consisted of a complete but crushed skull and a toe claw.

### Pocket fact

**Two Species!**
So far only two species of the Velociraptor have been discovered. One is Velociraptor mongoliensis, named in 1924 and the other is Velociraptor osmolskae, which was discovered in 2008.

### Find out

Why did the Stegosaurus have a throat guard?

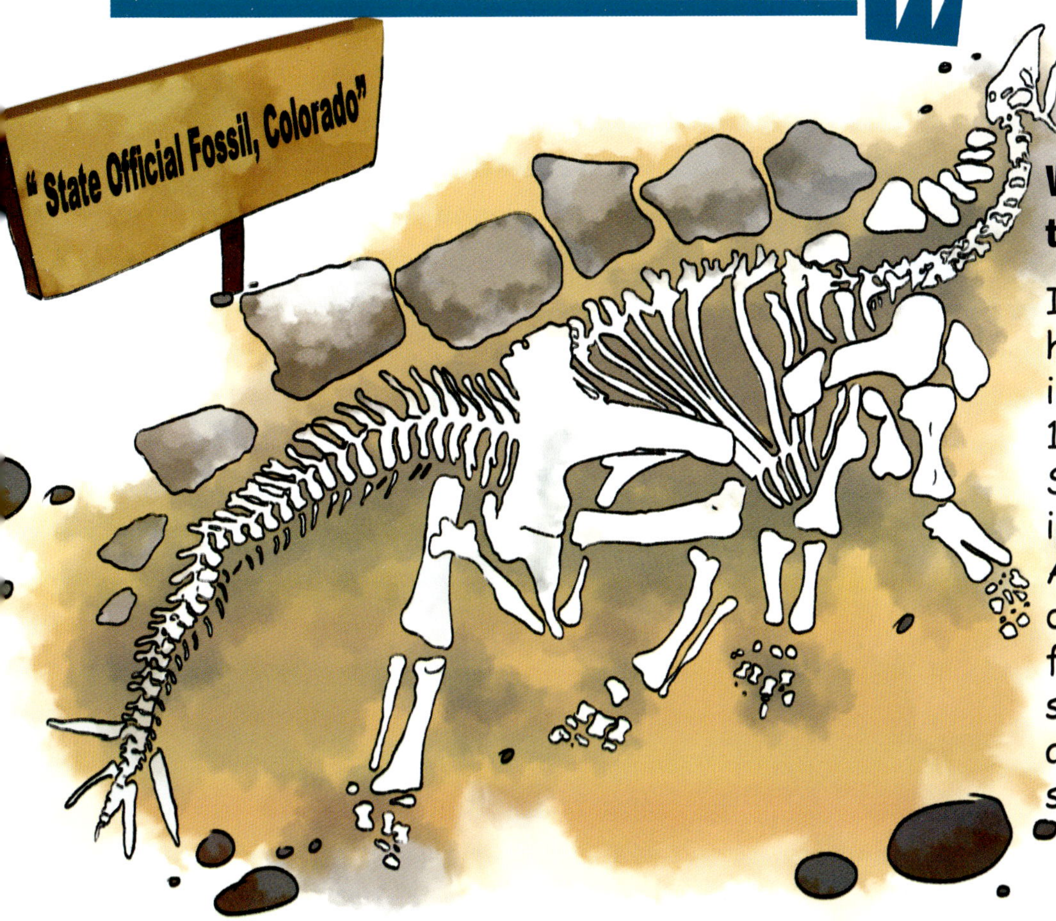


## When was the Stegosaurus declared the state fossil of Colorado?

In 1982! Stegosaurus was a large herbivorous dinosaur that lived in the area now called Colorado, 150 million years ago. The first Stegosaurus fossil was discovered in 1876, in Colorado, by M.P. Felch. Approximately 80 more fossils were discovered in the coming years. The fossils were declared the official state fossils of Colorado, in 1982, as a tribute to the number of dinosaur skeletons found in the state.

## When was the first longest dinosaur fossil found?

In 1877! Diplodocus was the longest of all known dinosaurs. The first Diplodocus fossil was found near Cañon City, Colorado in 1877. It was discovered by Benjamin Mudge and Samuel W. Williston, and was named by Othniel Charles Marsh in 1878. A number of Diplodocus fossils have also been found in the Rocky Mountain region of Colorado, Montana, Utah and Wyoming.

**Pocket fact**

**Laying eggs!**

In a surprising discovery, the palaeontologists discovered the eggs of the Diplodocuses in lines, rather than in nests. This suggests that these long Sauropods may have laid eggs while they walked along!

**Find out**

Which movie was entirely dedicated to dinosaurs? Which dinosaur was the most featured in this movie?

### When was the 'different lizard' discovered?

In 1877! Allosaurus, meaning 'different lizard,' was first discovered in Colorado in 1877, by palaeontologist Othniel Charles Marsh. This specimen comprised just a few fragments of the dinosaur's bones. These fragments were initially named Antrodemus and the family of these large theropods was named Allosauridae. But a study of the abundant remains from the Cleveland-Lloyd Dinosaur Quarry brought the name "Allosaurus" back to prominence.

## When was Dromaeosaurus discovered?

In 1914! The Dromaeosaurus was a small sized, lightly-built dinosaur that belonged to the family Dromaeosauridae. It flourished in Asia and North America during the Cretaceous period. The fossils of the Dromaeosaurus were first discovered by palaeontologist Barnum Brown, in the year 1914, along the banks of the Red Deer River of Alberta. In 1922, William Diller Matthew and Brown named this species—Dromaeosaurus albertensis. The generic name dromeus means 'runner' and sauros means 'lizard'. The specific name, "albertensis", refers to Alberta.

**Find out**

How long was the Dromaeosaurus?

**Pocket fact**

**The Alvarez hypothesis!**

The theory that the impact of a large asteroid hitting the Earth caused the mass extinction of dinosaurs and many other living things, was termed the Alvarez hypothesis. It is named after the father-and-son team of scientists, Luis and Walter Alvarez, who first suggested it in 1980.

### When did the rule of dinosaurs end?

About 65 million years ago! Dinosaurs ruled the Earth throughout the Mesozoic Era, approximately 245 million years ago, and vanished from Earth approximately 65 million years ago. The cause of their extinction remains a mystery with many reasons stated, such as climatic change, diseases, changing plant communities and geologic events. The most accepted theory is that a large asteroid struck the Earth, off the northern tip of the Yucatan Peninsula of Mexico; thus ending the rule of dinosaurs on Earth.

# Index